How to Self Publish a Kindle Book,

A Step-by-Step Guide

By Debra Shenkle

Other Books by Debra Shenkle:

The Color Wheel Made Easy
Silent Bonds

DEDICATION

To My Children, Siblings and SJ,

Whose love and devotion has been an incredible source of strength and encouragement for me to accomplish my big dreams.

INTRODUCTION

It seems that so many of us have big dreams of becoming a famous author selling our books worldwide and becoming a millionaire. Well, to Dream Big is the first step to any kind of success. If you want to become a millionaire or just write books as a hobby, Dreaming Big is what will continue to motivate you to reach your goals as a published author.

I have been dreaming big for most of my life and am just now reaching some of my Dream Big goals. One of my Big Dream goals was accomplished by becoming a published author in December 2011, when I published my first Kindle eBook. Writing that particular Kindle eBook was a project that I had been working on for several years. Actually, when I wrote my first eBook, **Vintage Ice Creams, Heirloom Recipes**, I had no plans of formatting and selling it in the Amazon Kindle eBook Store, but rather through other marketing venues.

One day a few months ago, I read one of those internet news stories about how so and so had made THOUSANDS of dollars in 6 months by selling her book on Amazon.com as a Kindle Edition eBook.

Admittedly, this sounded too good to be true, so I checked it out in the Amazon Kindle eBook Store and sure enough she did just that. A short novel that she submitted to many publishers but was rejected by them all, was suddenly making her a nice profit selling as a Kindle eBook.

This curiously sparked my interest in my eBook that had been sitting idle in a file on my personal computer for 3 ½ years! I decided to find out how this woman was able to self-publish her book to sell it in the Amazon Kindle eBook Store, what the publishing fees were and how I could get some instructions on self-publishing. With my renewed motivation it was time to resurrect my eBook from my computer file and begin the process of achieving the goal of self-publication and marketing through the Amazon Kindle eBook Store.

Devoting a complete 3-day weekend comprised of about 40 hours of internet research I suddenly felt confident enough in my abilities to complete the task at hand of self-publishing my eBook, **Vintage Ice Creams, Heirloom Recipes**, for sale as a Kindle eBook.

Of course, most people don't have that much time to devote to spend researching countless internet websites to accumulate the necessary tools to complete such a task. After the work week is over there is a plethora of tasks that must be accomplished over the weekend before returning to work on Monday morning, then starting it all over again .

I know that many of you would like to get your written works out there to be read and appreciated by millions of readers worldwide, not to mention the cash benefits of doing so. That is why I decided to assemble and write my second eBook, **How to Self-Publish a Kindle Book, A Step-by-Step Guide**.

It's time for you to start reaching your goals as a published author by starting or resurrecting and finishing your eBook to sell as a Kindle eBook in the Amazon Kindle eBook Store. By following this step-by-step guide you will be well on your way to success as an accomplished author read by a worldwide audience.

I'm not promising that you will become a millionaire, but maybe you will. With the age of technology at hand, I do feel that goal to be accomplishable, however. Think of this....Did you know that millions of additional Kindle Reader devices were sold just this past December? And, that doesn't include the millions of people that already owned Kindle Reader devices. What this means is that there are millions more people worldwide that now have access to buy, download and read Kindle eBooks. And, that doesn't count all of the other devices that can be used to read Kindle eBooks like smart phones including the iPhone, Blackberry, Android, Windows Phone 7, as well as, the iPad, and personal computers like Windows PC and

Apple MAC, etc. In other words, Kindle eBooks are virtually instantly   accessible to most persons in developed countries worldwide. With Kindle eBooks being available at such an affordable price they are very easily purchased by most readers.

Now I'm sure you are wondering how much it is going to set you back financially to self-publish your eBook to the Amazon Kindle eBook Store. Normally, self-publishing can be a very expensive venture and you must do all of the foot work yourself....meaning you have to do all of the sales and marketing of your book, as well.

Here is the really great part of self-publishing your book as a Kindle eBook....THERE ARE **NO,** YES I SAID **NO** upfront fees or costs to self-publish your eBook to sell in the Amazon Kindle eBook Store. Amazon has a few payment compensation options to choose from during the eBook downloading process. You set the price of your eBook, Amazon completes the purchase and payment process from the customer, then Amazon pays you a commission on the sale of your eBook. You can view your total eBook sales and commissions at any time by visiting your account at: **https://www. kdp.amazon.com**

With that being said, anyone with some basic computer and word processor knowledge (or with the help of someone that does) can publish an eBook to the Amazon Kindle eBook Store. It will require devoting a certain amount of time to writing your eBook, formatting and downloading it to the Kindle Direct Publishing website. However, it is an achievable goal even if you have only a small amount of free time to devote. Writing your eBook will take the majority of your time, but formatting it and downloading it to the Amazon Kindle eBook Store will take very little time at all.

If you find self-publishing a bit too challenging of a venture, do keep in mind that there are typesetting and formatting services available for a price. Such services will gladly prepare your book and download it to the Amazon Kindle eBook Store for you, if you desire. I for one, offer these services and would be glad to help you get your eBook typeset, proofed, edited, formatted and downloaded to the Amazon Kindle eBook Store. You will find my contact information in the ABOUT THE AUTHOR section of this book. Please feel free to contact me for a price quote.

It's time to GET READY, GET SET, and GO! You are now on your way to self-publishing bliss!

TABLE OF CONTENTS

WHAT YOU WILL NEED

You will need to have an **active** Amazon.com account in order to download Kindle eBooks for sale. If you do not have an active account with Amazon.com then the very first step is to navigate to the **http://www.amazon.com** home page where you will open and set up your account. It is important to complete the account setup process by including your income tax identification information so that Amazon can sell your Kindle eBook and compensate you for those that you do sell.

You must first be sure that you have a few software programs downloaded into your computer hard drive that are capable of accomplishing certain tasks necessary to the formatting of your eBook into the Kindle format. Here is a list of the current software programs that you will need to download before you begin to type your Kindle eBook:

FOR WINDOWS PC or MACINTOSH USERS: Make sure you have a good word processing software program installed into your computer that is capable of converting your text and photos into .**html** file format. There are many word processing software programs available but Amazon Kindle recommends Microsoft Word 7 or later as it seems to offer all of the appropriate features needed to create your Kindle eBook.

WORD PROCESSOR SOFTWARE
Microsoft Word for Windows PC or Apple Macintosh free 60-day trial or the paid version at:
http://www.microsoft.com/ download

TO PREVIEW YOUR KINDLE BOOK
Kindle Previewer for Windows PC or Apple Macintosh under the subheading **Tools and Resources** at: **http://www.kdp.amazon.com** Then navigate to **Tools and Resources**, Then **Self-Publishing Help** page. Or **http://www.amazon.com/kindleformat**

TO READ KINDLE BOOKS ON YOUR COMPUTER:

Free Kindle for Window PC and Apple Macintosh found in the **amazon.com** kindle book store.. Or at **http://www.amazon.com/gp/kindle/pc/download**

FILE CONVERTER SOFTWARE
Mobipocket Creator and Reader for Windows PC ONLY at:
http://www.mobipocket.com/en/downloadsoft

OR You may use either of the following programs to convert your files, but keep in mind that there are no instructions given in this guide for either of these so you will have to get the instructions from the websites listed:

KindleGen For Apple Macintosh or Windows PC users. If you are a computer programmer, you may enjoy using KindleGen as a command line tool for building a Kindle eBook. Use XHTML, HTML or EPUB files with Windows PC or Apple Macintosh at: **http://www.kdp.amazon.com** Then navigate to **Tools and Resources**, then to the **Self-Publishing Help** page.

Kindle Plugin for Adobe InDesign(v0.96) if you are planning to be creating your eBook in Adobe PDF file format. **http://www.amazon.com/kindleformat**

Amazon's Kindle Fire eBook reading devices have many new features including full color display. When downloading your eBook file into Amazon Kindle Direct Publishing, keep in mind that your images and text will display on the Kindle Fire in color, but all previous versions of Kindle in grayscale(b&w). All color photos, graphics and text that you include will be visible in color format on most other reading devices, however. I would recommend self-publishing a simple Kindle eBook as your first effort with limited photos and graphics. As you learn more about how Kindle Self-Publishing works you will be more comfortable self-publishing more reader interactive Kindle eBooks.

You can keep up with all updates and releases of all Kindle programs and devices by visiting:
http://www.amazon.com/kindlepublishing

TYPING YOUR EBOOK

Now you are ready to type your eBook into a word processing document that you will save on your computer for later converting into the Kindle file format. You must have a word processing software program installed into your computer that you can save into a **document** file that is capable of later being converted and saved into an **.html** file format.

There are many word processing software programs that are capable of converting your **document** files into **.html** format files, but Microsoft 7 Word or later seems to work very well for accomplishing those tasks and it is the Amazon Kindle recommended word processing software. Whatever word processing program that you do use, please be certain that is also capable of accomplishing those same tasks.

For simplicity sake and ease of use, the directions for typing and formatting your eBook will be given using Microsoft 7 Word for Windows PC. As you are typing your eBook please keep in mind that when your word processor document file is converted into the Kindle format, it will set up the pages differently. So it is important that you **do not** indent your paragraphs or center any type on your pages. Type them flush to the left margin of the page. **Do not** force your paragraphs using the left margin justification feature in your word processor.

Even though indentations and italics should translate well into the Kindle format, I did not find this to be the case. Bullets, special fonts and the like may not convert well into Kindle. However, the newest Kindle format KF8 claims to have solved these issues.

Separate each of your **paragraphs** with a **double line** space.
It is not necessary to type in page numbers as Kindle does not use your page numbers as references, so if you type them in, they will somewhat mess up the look of your Kindle eBook pages during the Kindle format converting process.

Also, you will have **to insert a page break at the end of each chapter** of your eBook to separate them so that the chapters do not run together. Do this immediately following the **last letter** of the **last word** in the **last sentence** of each chapter. This should be done **AFTER** you have completely typed the content of your Kindle eBook, have proofread, edited, and are satisfied with it.
Insert your Page Breaks by selecting **Insert** from your Word Processor page. Then select **Page Break**.

The following is an example of where your Page Breaks should be located throughout your eBook:

Title / Author Page (Page Break)
Copyright/Permissions Page (Page Break)
Dedication Page (Page Break)
Introduction/Preface Page (Page Break)
Prologue Page (Page Break)
Table of Contents Page (Page Break)
Body of Book Pages (Page Break at the **end of each chapter**)
References/Acknowledgements/Credits Page (Page Break)
About the Author (No Page Break at the End of the eBook)

Make sure that you have proofread your eBook and have made all necessary error corrections before you convert the **document** file content of your eBook to an **.html** file format. It is easy to miss your own typing errors if you are proofreading your own Kindle eBook content, so you may find it beneficial to have someone else read over it for you, as well. Some constructive criticism may help you avoid missing errors in your eBook and may give you an idea of how it will appeal to your readers.

Also, reading your eBook on an actual printed page makes it somewhat easier to locate any typing errors that you may miss while proofreading your manuscript in digital form on your computer. If you have a printer it may be beneficial for you to use it to print your eBook out on copy paper for additional proofreading.

The best way to help your readers find content in your eBook is to set up an **active** Table of Contents at the beginning of your eBook. That way your reader can simply select the chapter they desire to read and be taken directly to it when it is selected.

If you are planning to insert images into your Kindle eBook please keep in mind that you should only use very high definition **.jpeg** format images with a dpi(dots per inch) of at least **300** minimum. Do not copy and paste images into your Kindle eBook as these will not convert well into the Kindle format.

There are copyright laws that protect the author of any image they create so you will need written permission from the author before you can use any of their creative images in any your Kindle eBooks. The easiest solution to this is to either design it yourself, take your own images or pay someone else do it for you.

ORDER OF BOOK PAGES

It is important to organize your eBook into appropriate page categories. Place a **page break** at the end of each page so that they will not run together when your eBook is converted into the Kindle format. Following is a list showing the placement of your eBook pages:

TITLE PAGE
AUTHOR/ILLUSTRATOR
COPYRIGHT
DEDICATION
INTRODUCTION/PREFACE
PROLOGUE, if one
TABLE OF CONTENTS
BODY OF BOOK
REFERENCES/CREDITS
ABOUT THE AUTHOR/ACHIEVEMENTS

be a place where you will download a Digital Image of your Book Cover. When your eBook is opened in Kindle reading devices, your Book Cover will show as the first page of your eBook.

CREATING YOUR PAGES Step 1

The first page of your eBook will be the **Book Cover** page. This page will automatically be created for you during the downloading process of your eBook file into Kindle Direct Publishing (KDP).
During the downloading process there will be a place where you will download a Digital Image of your Book Cover. When your eBook is opened in Kindle reading devices, your Book Cover will show as the first page of your eBook.

TITLE PAGE Step 2

To begin typing your eBook, open the Word Processing program in your computer, then select, "Create Document." A blank document page will appear. This will be your **Title Page**. You will need to check to see if the type of font that is selected is compatible with the Kindle format. There should be a box in the upper left of your word processor page that shows what font you are using and the size of the font. Size **12 point** in **Times New Roman** is a dependable font choice.

Once you have done this, type the **Title Page** on the blank page that you have just created. Remember to include the name of your image designer and/or illustrator/photographer. Follow the example shown on the **Title Page** of this book.

Once, you have typed your **Title Page** information, press **Enter** on your keyboard to scale down the page until another blank page appears.

COPYRIGHT PAGE Step 3

This will be your **Copyright** page. Type it following the example of the Copyright Page of this book. Be sure to include any permissions or copy restrictions on this page.

SAVING YOUR WORK Step 4

Now would be a great time to start saving your precious work so as to prevent you from accidently losing your work. Follow these instructions if you do not know how to **save** your file to a **document file**. If you are using **Microsoft Word** you will save your file in a **Microsoft Word Document** file.

Click on the white **X** in the small **red** box in the upper right corner of the word processor page. A box will open asking you if you want to **save** or **don't save**. Select **save**. Then another box will appear asking you to **name** your file. Type in the name that you want to identify your eBook file with. Then select the **file format** that you want to save the file as. Select a **Microsoft Word Document** if you are using **Microsoft Word.** Then **click** the **save** button.

Now your eBook file is stored into your computer for later use. When you are ready to begin working on your eBook again, just **select** it from your document files. Remember, it is a good idea to **SAVE** your eBook file periodically while you are typing or adding images in order to prevent possible loss of your work accidently. Always, **save** your work when you are taking a break from it or finished with it for the day.

It never hurts to also save your file onto a Flash Drive just in case your computer would happen to crash for some reason. Then, at least you will still have a copy of your eBook available to download into another computer so that you can finish it without losing all of your valuable eBook content.

DEDICATION PAGE Step 5

Now, create a new blank page just as you have done with the other pages by pressing **Enter** on your keyboard until a new blank page appears. Then, you will type the **Dedication** page if you are including one in your eBook. Following is an example:

DEDICATED,
"To my Dear Husband, James, who tirelessly encouraged me in my pursuit of writing this book."

INTRODUCTION/PREFACE PAGE Step 6

After you have created the Dedication page of your eBook, you will create the **Introduction/Preface** to your eBook. These are pages where you will introduce your readers to your book. You do not always need an Introduction and/or Preface to your eBook as it depends on the content and type of book you are writing. Please refer to the introduction of this eBook as an example.

PROLOGUE PAGE Step 7

If you are including a **Prologue,** place that page immediately after the Introduction/Preface.

TABLE OF CONTENTS PAGE Step 8

When you design your **Table of Contents** page it is important to design it as an **active** Table of Contents so that your reader can simply select the chapter that they wish to begin reading and be taken to that chapter immediately. You will want to create your **active** Table of Contents page **after** you have typed and created all of the chapters with headings and all of the other pages of your eBook.

Some word processing programs have options available for you to insert an **active** Table of Contents into your document. Please follow the directions in your word processing program to create your active Table of Contents. Since each word processing program is designed differently, it would be impossible for me to instruct you on how each would work for you. Just remember to insert it into your **Table of Contents** page of your eBook. If you are not familiar with how to create an active Table of Contents, I would recommend creating a separate document where you can experiment with it before you actually create the Table of Contents in your eBook.

Following are instructions for creating an active Table of Contents in Microsoft Word:

Open your document in Word, then with your curser **select** the area on the page that you would like your active Table of Contents to appear in your document.

From the **Reference** tab Select **Table of Contents.** A box will appear. Then, select **Insert Table of Contents.** Another box will appear.

Next, **choose your options** by leaving the **check marked** boxes as is, or choose to deselect the checked options. Also, select your preferred **format** and also select the **levels** of your headings and subheadings. Then, Select **OK**.

A message will appear in the area that you selected for your Table of Contents saying, **"Error! No table of contents entries found."** Now, you are ready to start building your active Table of Contents.

Add each of your chapter headings by doing the following: **Locate** your first chapter heading with your curser then **highlight** it. Next, select **Home** from the options at the top of the Word processor page.

Then, in the **Styles** box, select the **Heading Style** (1 or 2), etc. After you have selected the Heading Style for your first chapter heading, locate your second chapter heading and **repeat** the process until you have done this to all of your chapter headings.

Now, select **References** at the top of the Word processing page. Select **Update Entire Table.** Your chapter headings should now appear in the Table of Contents area of your document that you earlier selected.

In the line above your first chapter entry, **Type** the words **Table of Contents**. Select **References**, then **Update Entire Table of Contents**. Then, erase the message "Error! No table of contents entries found."

Your active Table of Contents has now been created. To confirm its active status just hover the arrow on your screen over each of the chapter titles. Then follow the instructions shown to be taken directly to the chosen chapter.

Most word processing programs use a format similar to Word to build an active Table of Contents. In the **Reference** section of this Book you will find some helpful links to websites that have available tutorials on building an active Table of Contents.

If the word processing program that you are using to build your active Table of Contents is not listed in the Reference section of the Book, simply locate its website's main page to find **help** resources or tutorials. You may also be able design your **active** Table of Contents in the Mobipocket Creator while you are preparing to Build your eBook from an **.html** file into the **.prc** file format. Just **select** the option, **Table of Contents**, after you have loaded your Publication Files and Book Cover into the Mobipocket Creator. Fill in the appropriate information using corresponding words that will **link** the Table of Contents chapters to the Chapter Titles which are located throughout your eBook. In other words, if your chapter title is **Typing Your eBook**, then type in those same words into the active

Table of Contents in the Mobipocket Creator exactly the way it is shown in your eBook document.

Amazon recommends inserting an **active** Table of Contents into your Kindle eBook. However, it is not mandatory for you to insert an **active** Table of Contents into your eBook. You can just type a Table of Contents into your Table of Contents page if you would like. However, having an **active** Table of Contents will make your eBook easier to navigate by your readers, thus providing a more pleasant reading experience for them.

BODY OF YOUR EBOOK PAGES Step 9

Now you are ready to begin typing the **body** of your eBook. Create a new blank page to begin the **body** of your book. This is where you will type the actual content of your book which may include a compilation of many pages and chapters. Please refer to the suggestions given in the chapter, **Typing Your eBook**.

Remember to regularly **save** the contents of your eBook file to avoid the frustration of accidently losing your precious work. When you **save** your work to a file, remember to **save** it into a **document** file assigning it an easily recognizable file name. When you are ready to begin working on your eBook again simply open your documents files, then select your eBook file to open it. You can then resume typing your eBook by adding content or making corrections. Remember to **save** your changes and corrections immediately.

Type all content flush with the left margin, heading included. Type sentences single spaced and place a double space between each paragraph. During formatting Kindle will automatically intent the beginning of each paragraph for you. The double line space will indicate each new paragraph.

If you are using fractions in your eBook, you must type the actual fraction out as such: 1/2 or one-half but not using the special keyboard keys that will type that fraction. Otherwise it will not format correctly for Kindle and your readers will not be able to distinguish what the fraction actually is.

Continue this process until you have completed the body of your eBook. Remember to clearly label each chapter at the being of each new one.

REFERENCES/CREDITS PAGE Step 10

Once you have completely typed the body of your eBook, you can create your next page which is the **"References Credits Acknowledgments Resources"** page. Here you will list any information references and resources that you used to write your eBook giving the proper acknowledgements and credits to those necessary. Always remember to acquire the proper permissions from the sources that you are using or quoting information from

ABOUT THE AUTHOR PAGE Step 11

When you are finished with your **"References Credits Acknowledgements Resources"** page if you are including it, then it would be beneficial for you to create your **About the Author** page. This is the final page of your eBook and is very important because here is where you can give your reader some information about you, your accomplishments, your contact information and a photo of yourself if you would like. When you are finished with this page it is time to start adding any images that you want included in your eBook.

ADDING IMAGES Step 12

You can make your eBook more interesting to your readers by including images throughout the content of your eBook. Images can be either digitally created or they can be pictures that you have digitally photographed. All images must be of a minimum size of

600x800 pixels and 300dpi. You will either need to create your own images or pay someone else do it for you.

You will then need to download and save the **.jpeg** images into your computer **picture** files. Once you have accomplished this task you can simply add these images into selected areas of your eBook as follows:

Locate the area in your eBook where you want your image to appear by using your curser. Select **Insert** from the top of your word processor page. Then, select **Insert Pictures from file**. Your pictures and images will then appear. Select the **image** that you want to insert into your eBook. After the image appears in the selected area of your eBook, you may need to scale down the size of it by using the arrows located in the corner of the image until you reach the desired size. Continue adding the remaining images to your eBook.

You are almost finished creating your eBook. Once you have finished a couple of final steps, your eBook will be ready for Kindle formatting.

DESIGNING YOUR EBOOK COVER Step 13

Your **Book Cover** is one of the most important aspects of creating your eBook because the cover is what your readers will first see when they browse through the Amazon Kindle Store eBook selections. So, take some time when you create your **Book Cover** keeping in mind the content of your eBook and what image you want to convey to your reader. The **Book Cover** can actually **sell** your book if done correctly.

You can easily design your own **Book Cover** if you have some basic knowledge of a graphic design program. Many use fancy graphic design programs which are fine. Others use simpler graphic design programs which can be downloaded free from the internet onto your computer (See chapter, **What You Will Need**), or others simply hire a Graphic Arts Designer to create a Book Cover. Hiring a graphic arts designer can get a little pricey but it may save you some frustration if you are not familiar with how to use a graphic art software program and do not want to invest the time to learn how to use one.

Your eBook Cover Image will be added during the process of downloading your .prc file into Kindle Direct Publishing.

Now that you have added all of the content to your eBook, have made all necessary corrections and are completely satisfied with it, you are ready for the final steps of creating your eBook.

CREATING AN ACTIVE TABLE OF CONTENTS Step 14

Your **active TABLE OF CONTENTS** needs to be created so that your readers can easily navigate throughout your eBook. Follow the directions found in **Step 8, Table of Contents** section of this Book .

PLACING PAGE BREAKS Step 15

After you have satisfactorily finished creating the active **Table of Contents** and are happy with all aspects of your eBook it's time to place your **Page Breaks**. Place the appropriate **Page Breaks** after each chapter of your eBook. Please refer to the chapter, **Typing Your eBook**, for instructions on how to place your **Page Breaks**.

Before you place your Page Breaks, eliminate all blank areas of your eBook, such as empty pages. Now, you are ready to place your Page Breaks.

After you have placed your Page Breaks, review your eBook to be certain that there are NO empty pages. If you find any empty pages, eliminate those pages.

ADDING BOOKMARKS Step 16

Amazon Kindle has an option called **Go To** which will immediately take the reader of your eBook to specific areas of your eBook such as the Beginning of the eBook and the Table of Contents. To activate this feature you must design it into your original eBook document file following this example:

To add a Bookmark to the beginning of your eBook, place your curser on the **first letter** of the beginning paragraph of your eBook, then select **Insert**. From Insert, select **Bookmark**. Type the word, **Start** in dialogue box, then select **Add**.

To Bookmark your Table of Contents, place your curser on the first letter of the first entry(chapter) of your Table of Contents. Select **Insert,** Then Select **Bookmark**. In the Bookmark name field type, **Contents.** Then, Select **Add.** These are the two places in your eBook that you typically need to place Bookmarks.

ADDING CROSS REFERENCES Step 17

The Word Processor that you are using to type and design your eBook will no doubt include a feature that you can use to **Cross Reference** pages, headings or words. You can open and use this feature within your eBook by selecting **References** and then **Cross Reference** from the options found at the top of your word processor page.

There are many other features at your disposal in your word processing program that will definitely be useful to you as you design your eBook. If you aren't already familiar with the features provided in your word processor, you may find it beneficial to take a little time to become familiar with them. Including some of these added features in your eBook will give your reading audience a more pleasant reading experience.

Congratulations! Your eBook is officially finished! Pat yourself on the back, celebrate or do something to reward yourself for all of your hard earned efforts.

CONVERTING TO .HTML Step 18

Now that your eBook is finished, it's entire contents is ready to be formatted into a file type called a **.prc** file that can be downloaded into the Amazon Kindle eBook Store. In order to create a **.prc** file of your eBook, you must **first** create an **.html** file of the entire contents of your eBook. This process requires your word processor program to convert your eBook's Microsoft Word Document file into an .**html** file.

To do this simply **Open** your eBook file in your word processor, Select **File** from the upper left side of the page. From there Select **Save as**. Then, in the **Save as** box Select **Webpage Filtered** which is actually .**html** from the drop down file options by **clicking** on the arrow on the right side of the box if you are working in Microsoft Word. Then, simply select **Save**. Now you will have two differently formatted files of your eBook saved into your document files. One will be your original document file and the other will be the newly created **.html** file of your eBook. All of your images will be saved in a separate folder in your document files. That file will be identified as a **folder** file.

It may be beneficial to also save a PDF file of your eBook so that you can email someone a copy of it if desired. You can easily do this from the **save as** file option in your word processor, by following the same steps that you saved a copy of your eBook as an .html file earlier. A PDF file can be read by anyone that has Adobe Reader downloaded into their computer or smart phone, etc. Most computer or smart phone owners will have Adobe Reader available for use to read your eBook. A free version of

Adobe Reader is available for download at: **http://www.adobe.com**
.

CONVERTING TO .PRC Step 19

Now that you have converted your eBook file to a **.html** file, you will further need to change the **.html** file to a **.prc** file. For simplicity purposes the instructions in this guide are for using Mobipocket Creator to convert your **.html** file into a **.prc** file. Mobipocket Creator is pretty quick and easy to navigate and is also compatible with the Kindle format, so that is why I prefer to use it over the other file converting tools available.

However, you can also convert your eBook file from a **.PDF** file to a Kindle file format by using the Kindle Plugin for Adobe InDesign.

Also, a command line tool called KindleGen will convert **HTML,XHTML** or **EPUB** files into the Kindle eBook file format.

KindleGen and Kindle Plugin for Adobe Design can be downloaded free with instructions for use at:
http://kdp.amazon.com/selfpublishing.

Apple Macintosh users will need to use **KindleGen** for the .html to .prc file conversion. Since I am not a Macintosh user and am not familiar with how to use KindleGen as of yet, I cannot offer you any instructions on how to use it. There are instructions for its use on the Amazon.com website found at:
http://www.amazon.com/gp/feature.html under the subheading, Kindle Publishing Guidelines. Also, please note that KDP(Kindle Direct Publishing) does support zipped .html files, .doc files, .ePub files, .txt(plain text), .PDF files, and .rtf(Rich Text Format)files. However, uploading these types of files will limit optimum usability when viewed on Kindle reading devices. They may only be used with simple formatted files. Complicated files with certain types of tables, various fonts, and many images, etc. will need to be converted using KindleGen before downloading to the KDP format.

KDP highly recommends converting your eBook file into the .prc file format before uploading to KDP for optimum usability on Kindle reading devices. For more information on **Types of Formats**, refer to the Help Topics guide found at:
http://www.kdp.amazon.com/self-publishing/help

If you are using **Windows PC**, the instructions for converting your **.html** eBook file into a **.prc** file using the Mobipocket Creator are as follows:

First, locate the Mobipocket Creator that you downloaded earlier to your computer(See the chapter, **What You Will Need**). It will either be located in a shortcut folder on your **desktop** or it will be listed in your **All Programs** list.

Open the Mobipocket Creator. Under the Heading, **Import From Existing File** select **HTML document** from the options displayed. A box called **Import File Wizard** will appear.

Next, the **Choose a File** box will be displayed which will be empty. Select **browse** located to the right of the empty box. Your file **Library** will open.

Then, select **documents.** All of the documents that are stored in your computer will be displayed in a list according to the name that has been assigned to them.
Locate your **.html** eBook file and double click on it. The file name and location will then be displayed in the **Choose a File** box. Select **Import**.

The eBook editing function will then open a new page called, **Publication Files** showing the name of the **.html** eBook file that you just downloaded.

Now, from the options under **View**, select **Cover Image**. This will take you to your Library of files.

Select **Documents.** Then, select the folder where your images are stored. This will be a file called **folder** identified with the name that you assigned to your original eBook file.

Select the **image** that you want displayed as your eBook cover, if you have one. A new page will open showing the image that you uploaded. Select **Update** to add the image as your Book Cover.

If you have not yet included an active Table of Contents in your eBook using your word processor program, it may be possible to add one at this point if you would like. I say, may, because many people are having problems creating a Table of Contents using the Mobipocket Creator. Some information suggests that it works fine using Internet Explorer 8 but that it doesn't work at all using Internet Explorer 9. Since I use Internet Explorer 9 it wouldn't work for me. Therefore, I can offer no instructions on how to create an active Table of Contents using Mobipocket Creator. If you decide to try it out, I would recommend creating a test document converted into an .html file as a sample to use rather than your actual eBook.

In **Book Settings** under Book Type select **eBook**. This is actually a **.prc** or **Kindle Content** file. All other setting should be left alone **as is** in the default setting chosen by Mobipocket Creator.

Select **Metadata** from list of options under **View**. Fill in all of the necessary information being sure to also add your Book Cover image, again. Now you are ready to actually build your eBook by converting the **.html** file into a **.prc** file.

To do this select **Build** from the toolbar located at the top of the page. A new page will appear called **Build Publication**. Leave all settings as they are, in the **default mode**, but **make certain that Standard Compression and No Encryption are selected.**

Select **Build**. When your eBook is finished building or converting the files into **.prc** file format, a new window will display **Build Finished**.

Select **Open folder containing eBook**. Then select **OK**. This will take you to the document file folder where your eBook is located. Notice that the type of file is now an **eBook file or Kindle Content file**. It will be stored in the **My eBooks** or **My Kindle** folder in your Documents Library.

Now, **Close** all open windows. It's time to preview your eBook so that you can confirm that it will appear correctly on the Kindle device and other compatible devices. To do this **Open** the Kindle Previewer or Kindle Reader(See chapter, **What You Will Need**), located in your programs list in your computer.

Select **File**. Then select **Open Book**. A list of your eBooks will appear. Select your **eBook** or **Kindle Content** file. **Select** your eBook from the Kindle eBook list of books, then click on it to open into the Kindle Previewer or Kindle Reader. From there you will be able to see what your newly created eBook will look like when it is read by your audience.

If you find that you need to make further corrections to your eBook, simply **open** your original eBook document file (Microsoft Word Document). **Make** your changes, then **save** your changes. **Open** your corrected document file, then **save** it to an **.html** file as you did previously.

Then, download the corrected **.html** file into the Mobipocket Creator. Follow all of the steps again. Preview it again in the Kindle Previewer or Kindle Reader.

When your eBook is satisfactory, you will be ready to finally download your eBook file into KDP(Kindle Direct Publishing) for sale in the Amazon Kindle eBook Store. Keep in mind that your eBook may not look perfect on the Kindle Previewer or may not display as perfectly as you would like on Kindle reading devices. Do the best you can to remedy any problems in the display of your eBook, but accept that it may never be perfect no matter what you do to try to remedy some problems.

Please be sure that you have opened an Amazon.com account and have filled in all of the information required, prior to downloading your eBook into KDP.

DOWNLOADING TO KDP Step 20

Now that you have your eBook formatted into a .prc file, it is ready to be downloaded for sale as a Kindle eBook in the Amazon Kindle eBook Store. To do this simply navigate to the Kindle Direct Publishing website page at: **https://kdp.amazon.com**

Sign in with your Amazon account. Once you have signed in you will be taken to the Kindle Direct Publishing page. You will be given the option to read about the KDP Select program before you download your Kindle eBook for sale. It's important that you read about the KDP Select program before you download your Kindle eBook for sale because you will be given an option to join this program as you are going through the process of downloading your Kindle eBook. Keep in mind, that **if** you join the KDP Select program, your Kindle eBook will be tied up in the program for 90 days and you will only be able to offer your Kindle book for free to reviewers or anyone else on a limited 5-day time frame during the next 90 days. There is complete information about the KDP Select program are various places found on the Kindle Direct Publishing Pages. Please read this information carefully before you make a choice to join it or not.

The KDP home page offers a wealth of publishing benefits. Helpful links can be accessed within KDP through the link buttons found at the top of the page. Exploring these links will provide you with many resources of Helpful and Useful information that are at your disposal to you as a Kindle author.

The next step is to click on the **Add New Title** button. You will be taken to the beginning of the Kindle eBook download. Fill in the form following the instructions found with each step. Since you won't have an ISBN # for your Kindle eBook yet, do not enter anything into that box. Instead, Amazon will create an **ASIN** # for your Kindle eBook as it is being downloaded. During the download process you will be asked to set the price of your Kindle eBook. Be sure to read about how you will be paid commissions on your Kindle eBook before you set your Kindle eBook price. There will be options on each page of the download process where you can read about it and about other subjects relating to your Kindle eBook. Most persons find it beneficial to list their new Kindle eBook titles at a fairly low price somewhere between $0.99 to $3.99, so that they can get their sales to start taking off. However, you will be given several pricing options.

Be sure that you understand the pricing and commissions guidelines before you enter a price and commission choice. Once a large amount of sales have been enjoyed, the price of your Kindle eBook and commission amount can be increased or adjusted using the editing option on the main KDP Direct Publishing page. Of course, you can always adjust your Kindle eBook price and commission amount at any time by using the edit option on the main KDP Direct Publishing.

Once you have finished the process of downloading your Kindle eBook, it will appear within the next 24 hours for sale in the Amazon Kindle eBook Store. Amazon will send you an email confirming that your Kindle eBook has been published to the Amazon Kindle eBook Store. You can check out your new Kindle eBook by doing a search in the Amazon Kindle eBook Store at:
http://www.amazon.com

To keep track of your Kindle eBook sales and commissions, you can just go to the Kindle Direct Publishing home page from: **https://kdp.amazon.com** to view your sales and commissions. From the KDP home page select **Reports** to be directed to your book sales pages. After you have downloaded your eBook to KDP you may decide to offer a print edition of your book at some point. Amazon offers CreateSpace.com as a means for self-publishers to create and offer their books in print form. It works much the same way as KDP, but is a bit more complicated. However, once you have successfully created your eBook into a print book through CreateSpace, then it can be linked up to appear with your eBook on Amazon.com. After that you will find the option in your KDP editing pages to offer your digital edition at a discount to customers who buy the print version also. You will find this option setting on the last page of the your eBooks editing pages in KDP.

COPYRIGHTING YOUR BOOK

It is always beneficial to have your eBook Copyrighted to avoid infringement upon your written works. Copyrighting your eBook can be done in one of two ways. You can either apply for a Copyright by filling out an online form and submitting a digital copy of your eBook or you can apply by snail mail submitting a printed hard copy. Either way you will need to visit the U.S. Copyright website to either submit it online or to print out a form to mail in with a copy of your eBook. You will find everything that you need to know about Copyrighting your eBook at: **http://www.copyright.gov**

MARKETING

After you have downloaded your eBook to the Amazon Kindle eBook Store, you will need to do some Marketing so that the world will know that it is available for purchase. Marketing will take some time and patience. There are many ways that you can market your Kindle eBook. Some authors have found that using a variety of Social Networks to market their eBooks has been very valuable to their Kindle eBook sales.

There is a wide variety of Social Networking websites available for use. Doing an online search will yield a large selection to choose from. Promoting your Kindle eBook through as many as possible will be very beneficial to your Kindle eBook sales.

Amazon offers you the option of creating an Author Profile page to accompany your Kindle eBook(s) page and for you to use for

marketing. Once you have successfully listed your eBook in the Amazon Kindle Book Store, visit:
https://authorcentral.amazon.com to set up your author page. There you will find other resources for marketing you Kindle eBooks. Some popular websites are:

http://www.shelfari.com
https://www.createspace.com
http://www.facebook.com
https://twitter.com
http://www.stumbleupon.com
http://flickr.com
http://pinterest.com
http://www.linkedin.com
http://www.myspace.com
http://www.youtube.com
http://google.com
https://www.plus.google.com (for Google +1)
Wikipedia offers s large list of some popular Social Networking website.
http://en.wikipedia.org/wiki/List_of_social_networking_websites

You may also find it beneficial to open a free Blog account where you can write an article introducing your Kindle eBook. From there you can share it with the world using some of the most popular Social Networking websites. Setting up a simple Blog will take a little of your dedicated time. However, a more complicated Blog will most generally take a significant amount of time, especially if you include ads and links to other websites on your blog pages. Find websites that offer Blog Creating by doing an internet search or by using one of the more popular free Blog Creating websites that can be found at:
http://www.blogger.com
http://wordpress.com

Another very effective marketing tool is the use of Consumer Product Reviews. Obviously, great reviews will bring you more sales. Getting great reviews can be somewhat time consuming but definitely worth the time you can invest into finding persons willing to read your eBook, then leaving a review of it at the Amazon Kindle eBook Store page where your eBook is located for sale. Amazon offers the reviewer the option of rating your Kindle eBook with the "5 star" system. Without any reviews, your Kindle eBook will probably not sell very well, so it is very important to get some "5 star" reviews as quickly as possible after you list your Kindle eBook for sale in the Amazon Kindle eBook Store.

There are websites that offer consumer product review services. **Blogvertise.com** and **tomason.com** among others, offer consumer product reviews by charging the producer of the product a small amount in exchange for soliciting their members to do a review of your product. Generally, you provide the reviewer with a free copy of your product or in this case, a short version of your eBook, then the reviewer writes a review of your product or eBook according to your requests. You may request that they write an article on their blog with a link to your Amazon Kindle eBook Store page and/or also leave a review on that page as well. You set the rules for the review and both websites have varying price scales for their services, which are usually pretty low.

Another way you can get some great reviews on your Amazon Kindle eBook page is to just ask your relatives, friends and acquaintances if they would like a free copy of your eBook in exchange for a review. Most persons will be eager to receive a free copy of your Kindle eBook, but you may need to check your Amazon Kindle eBook Store page periodically to see if they actually did leave the review and give them a gentle nudge if they haven't done so in the agreed upon time frame.

Once you have a couple of reviews listed on you Amazon Kindle eBook Store page, you will notice that you will begin to experience eBook sales. Even though your sales may start slow they may continue to rise as the months go by. However, you may need to consistently market your eBook for sales to continue.

You are now a Published Author, a cherished accomplishment. May I extend my Congratulations to you and may you enjoy Happy Writing and Happy Sales for many years to come.

Best Wishes,
Debra

RESOURCES/REFERENCES

WORD PROCESSOR SOFTWARE
Microsoft Word for Windows PC or Apple Macintosh free 60-day trial or the paid version at:
http://www.microsoft.com/download

TUTORIALS, How-to Articles, Demos, Videos, Templates.
Microsoft Word 2007/2010
http://office.microsoft.com/en-us/word-help
Microsoft Support 1-800-986-4316

GRAPHIC DESIGN SOFTWARE
Gimp 2 at: **http://www.gimp.org/downloads**
Or another graphic design program.

TO PREVIEW YOUR KINDLE BOOK
Kindle Previewer for Windows PC or Apple Macintosh under the subheading Tools and Resources,
Self-Publishing Help at: **http://www.kdp.amazon.com**
Or **http://www.amazon.com/kindleformat**

KINDLE READER FOR YOUR COMPUTER
Kindle for Window PC and Apple Macintosh under the subheading Tools and Resources, Self-
Publishing Help at:
http://www.kdp.amazon.com or
http://www.amazon.com/gp/kindle/pc/download

FILE CONVERTER SOFTWARE
Mobipocket Creator and Reader for Windows PC at:
http://www.mobipocket.com/en/downloadsoft

KindleGen if you are a computer programmer you may enjoy using KindleGen as a command line tool for building a more complicated Kindle book. Use XHTML, HTML or EPUB files with Windows PC

or Apple Macintosh. Download from the subheading Tools and Resources, Self-Publishing Help page
at**: http://www.kdp.amazon.com**
Kindle Plugin for Adobe InDesign(v0.96) if you are planning to be creating your eBook in Adobe PDF
file format. **http://www.amazon.com/kindleformat**
Amazon **http://www.amazon.com**
http://www.kdp.amazon.com/self-publishing/help

Adobe **Reader http://www.adobe.com**

Wikipedia
http://en.wikipedia.org/wiki/List_of_social_networking_websites

Google Blogspot **http://www.blogger.com**

Wordpress **http://wordpress.com**

ABOUT THE AUTHOR

Debra Shenkle was born and raised in the Heartland of the USA. After graduating from high school, married, had children and then moved to Southern California where she was instrumental in the building and inspection of the first Space Shuttle. Debra later moved back to the Midwest where she received her Associates Degree in Applied Arts and Sciences, then worked as a professional for many years. She now enjoys sharing her knowledge with others by authoring instructional books and videos. Debra also enjoys helping others get their books published by either offering instructions on self-publishing or by providing publishing services to them.

For more information on Over-the-Phone or In-Person Instructional Sessions for: Self-publishing your book to Amazon Kindle, CreateSpace, or help with creating or designing a blog on Blogspot Blogger, or for Information on Professional Proofreading Services Please Contact Debra at Ph:712-229-2039 or email her at: shenkle.books@gmail.com.

Debra's websites and contact information:
Email: **shenkle.books@gmail.com**
       dlodestein@yahoo.com
       uniquecozytreasures@gmail.com
Blog: **http://debshenkle.blogspot.com**
Blog: **http://uniquecozytreasures.blogspot.com**
Blog: **http://www.debsdogblogg.blogspot.com**
Twitter: **http://twitter.com/uniquecozy**
Handmade Items & Vintage Finds:
http://www.etsy.com/shop/uniquecozytreasures
http://www.youtube.com/videohomeandgarden.
Ph: 712-229-2039 M-F 9a-6p CTS.